JBIOG
Ford 04-9-08
Shores, Erika L.

Henry Ford : a photo-illustrated biography

Henry Ford

A Photo-Illustrated Biography

by Erika L. Shores

Consultant:
Catherine Klingman
Curator
Detroit Historical Museum

Bridgestone Books
an imprint of Capstone Press
Mankato, Minnesota

Bridgestone Books are published by Capstone Press
151 Good Counsel Drive, P.O. Box 669, Mankato, Minnesota 56002
http://www.capstone-press.com

Library of Congress Cataloging-in-Publication Data
Shores, Erika L., 1976–
    Henry Ford : a photo-illustrated biography / by Erika L. Shores.
        p. cm.—(Photo-illustrated biographies)
    Summary: Introduces the man who changed the American way of life in the
1900s by inventing the Model T and founding the Ford Motor Company.
    Includes bibliographical references and index.
    ISBN 0-7368-2223-2 (hardcover)
    1. Ford, Henry, 1863-1947—Juvenile literature. 2. Ford, Henry, 1863-1947—Pictorial
works—Juvenile literature. 3. Automobile industry and trade—United States
Biography—Juvenile literature. [1. Ford, Henry, 1863-1947. 2. Industrialists. 3. Automobile
industry and trade—Biography.] I. Title. II. Series.

TL140.F6S53 2004
338.7'6292'092—dc21   2002155880

Editorial Credits
Enoch Peterson, production designer; Kelly Garvin, photo researcher; Eric Kudalis, product
    planning editor

Photo Credits
Corbis/Bettmann, 14
From the Collections of Henry Ford Museum & Greenfield Village, cover, 6, 8, 10, 12, 16, 20
Stock Montage, Inc., 4, 18

1 2 3 4 5 6 08 07 06 05 04 03

Table of Contents

"Every man should make enough money to own a home, a piece of land, and a car."
–Henry, in a 1944 interview

Henry Ford

In the early 1900s, Henry Ford built the Model T car. This car changed the way millions of Americans lived. Owning a car allowed people to move from place to place easily. People could travel faster and work farther from their homes.

Henry did not invent the automobile. But he did make many important changes to the car industry. Henry started the Ford Motor Company. The company used mass production and the moving assembly line to make automobiles. Cars were made quickly and at a low cost using these systems.

Henry's changes to the car industry left a lasting mark on the United States. Henry's hard work made it possible for many people to own a car. Today, people continue to buy cars with the Ford name on them.

Henry Ford changed the American way of life when he invented the Model T car.

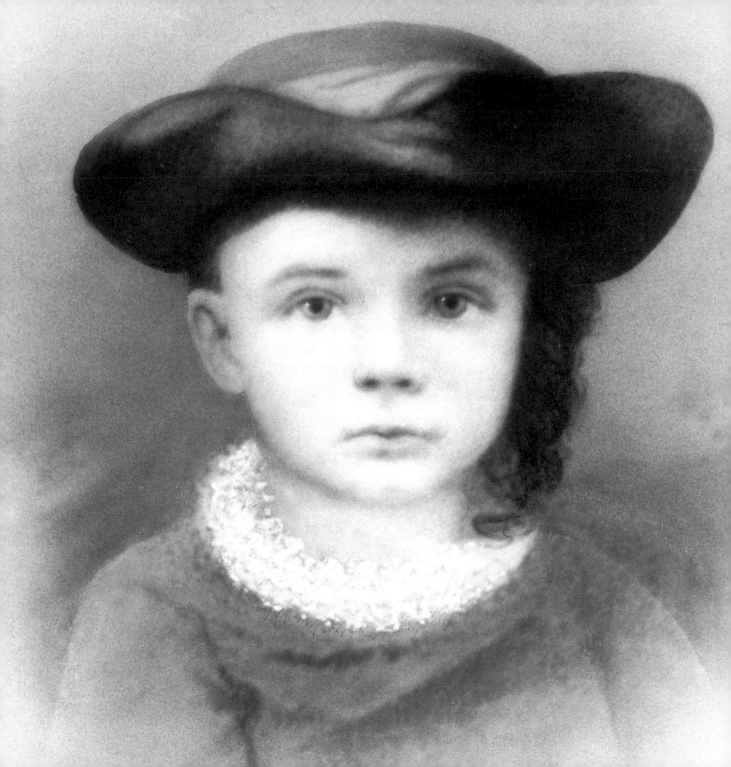

Early Years

Henry Ford was born July 30, 1863. He was the oldest of William and Mary Ford's six children. The Fords lived on a farm near Dearborn, Michigan.

Henry began school when he was 7 years old. Each day, he walked to a one-room schoolhouse. Henry had little interest in his schoolwork. He instead wanted to study the machines and tools on the family farm. He often took apart the farm machines and tools to see how they worked.

Farm machines were not the only things Henry took apart. Henry enjoyed studying toys and watches. Henry's brothers and sisters often hid their new toys from him. They did not want Henry to take the toys apart and break them. As he grew older, Henry earned money by fixing watches for his neighbors.

Young Henry was interested in machines and tools.

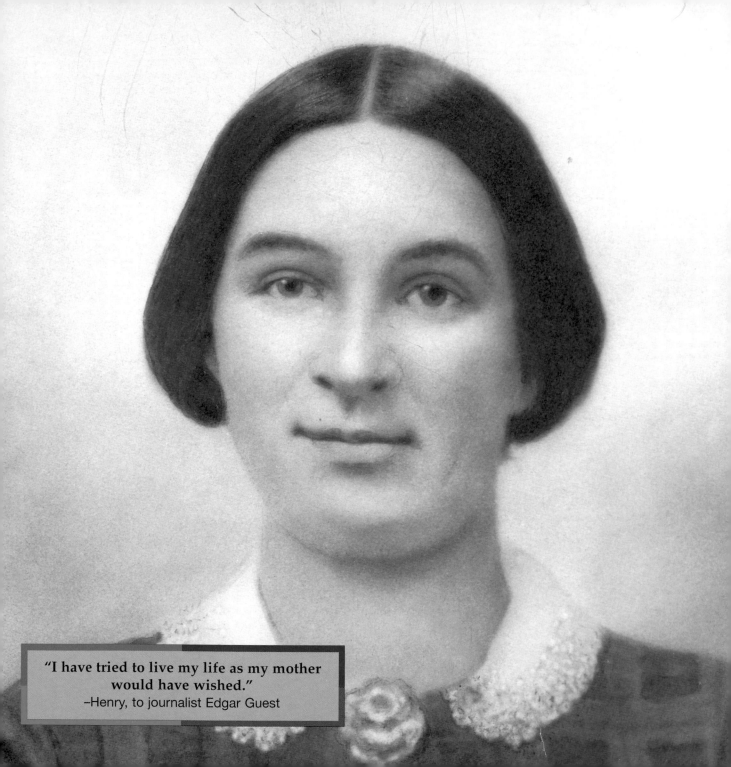

"I have tried to live my life as my mother
would have wished."
–Henry, to journalist Edgar Guest

Henry's Life Changes

Henry's life changed when he was only 13 years old. His mother died March 29, 1876. Henry was very sad. He was close to his mother. Later in life, Henry said the lessons his mother had taught him made him successful.

Another important event in Henry's life happened in July 1876. Henry and his father traveled to Detroit. On the way to Detroit, Henry saw a steam engine for the first time. This machine could move without horses pulling it. Henry decided he wanted to make a "horseless carriage" in which people could ride.

Henry wanted to work with machines. His father wanted him to be a farmer. Henry hoped to do more than work on the farm. At age 16, he left his Dearborn home. Henry walked 9 miles (14.5 kilometers) to Detroit.

Mary Ford wanted Henry to learn about the things that interested him.

Work and Marriage

Henry's interest in machines helped him find work in Detroit. He began working at a Detroit machine shop in 1879. In 1882, Henry fixed steam engines for Westinghouse Company. Later that year, Henry left Detroit and returned to his father's farm near Dearborn.

On April 11, 1888, Henry married Clara Bryant. Henry called Clara "the Believer." She believed he could invent a horseless carriage. Henry and Clara lived in Dearborn where Henry ran a sawmill.

Twenty-eight-year-old Henry got a job with the Detroit Edison Illuminating Company in 1891. He worked on steam engines that made electricity. Henry and Clara moved to Detroit. In 1893, they had their first and only child, Edsel.

Clara Bryant believed in Henry's dreams to build a horseless carriage.

Henry's First Car

Henry did not forget his dream of building a horseless carriage. He set up a workshop in a shed near his house. He wanted to build a small engine that burned gasoline. Henry planned to make a car that could move using the engine.

Henry worked on his car almost every evening and weekend. Henry's neighbors called him "Crazy Henry" because he spent so much time in the shed.

On June 4, 1896, Henry completed his Quadricycle. This machine had four wheels. It had two speeds and could only move forward. The only problem was that Henry's car was too big to fit through the shed door. Henry grabbed an axe and smashed the shed's doorframe and bricks. Finally, Henry could drive his "horseless carriage" out of the shed and through the city.

On June 4, 1896, Henry drove his Quadricycle through the streets of Detroit.

Henry's Company

In 1903, Henry started a small factory called the Ford Motor Company. The Model A was the first automobile the company made and sold.

Henry wanted everyone in the United States to be able to own a car. In 1908, Henry was ready to sell the Model T. This car cost $825. The Model T was easy to care for and operate. Still, Henry thought the price of the Model T was not yet low enough.

In 1913, the Ford Motor Company began using a moving assembly line. A car frame was placed on a large moving belt. Other moving belts carried parts to the workers building the cars. The workers stayed in one place. They fitted one part to each car frame moving past them on the line. This way of making cars was fast. By 1914, one Model T was made every 93 minutes at Henry's company. The price of the Model T fell to $550.

The Model T sold for $550 in 1914.

"As long as I live, I want to pay the highest wages in the automobile industry. If the men in our plants will give a full day's work for a full day's pay, there is no reason why we can't always do it."
–Henry, in a 1944 interview

Making Changes

Henry and his company continued making changes from 1914 to 1927. These steps helped keep costs low and increased the production of automobiles.

Henry knew hardworking employees would raise the number of cars made at the company. In 1914, Henry raised the minimum wage to $5 a day for his employees. Workers at other places received much less money. Many people wanted to work for Henry's company. He was able to hire the best workers.

The Ford Motor Company soon built a complex near the Rouge River in Dearborn. The complex had a steel mill, a glass factory, and an assembly line. Production costs were low because everything needed to make cars was in one place. By 1924, the Model T's price was down to $290. The average U.S. family could afford a Model T.

Henry stands on the banks of the Rouge River. The Ford Motor Company built a complex near the river.

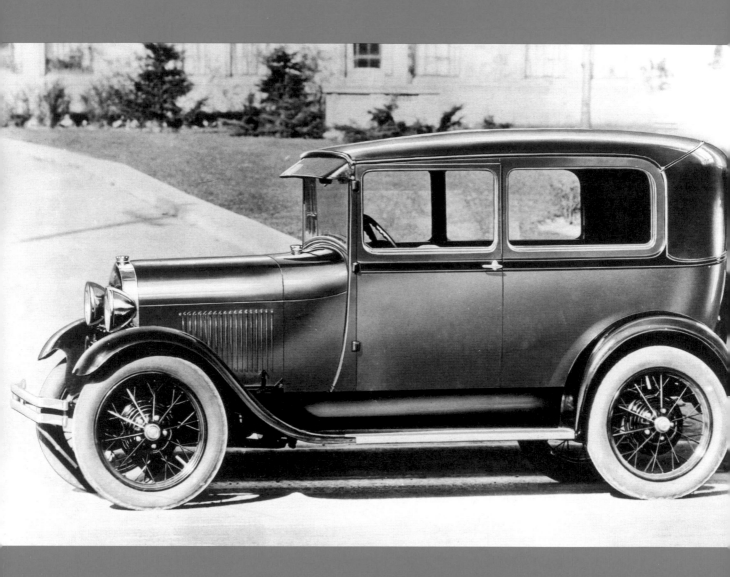

The End of the Model T

By 1925, sales of the Model T began to slow down. Henry refused to make changes to the Model T. It came only in black. Other car companies, such as General Motors, sold several models in different colors and with many features.

Henry's son, Edsel, had become the president of Ford Motor Company in 1919. Edsel knew the company needed a new car to boost sales. He asked Henry to stop making the Model T. In 1927, Henry watched the last Model T roll off the assembly line. It was the 15 millionth Model T ever made.

Ford Motor Company began to sell a new Model A in December 1927. The new Model A came in four different colors. The company sold many new cars. Once again, the Ford Motor Company was a leading car maker in the United States.

The Model A became a best-selling car for the Ford Motor Company.

Henry's Success

Henry's success with the Ford Motor Company made him very rich. In 1914, he and Clara moved to a large home outside Dearborn. They called their estate Fair Lane. Henry enjoyed living at Fair Lane. He often took long walks to watch the birds that lived near his home.

Henry was interested in history and items from the past. In 1929, he opened the Henry Ford Museum and Greenfield Village in Dearborn. The museum and village includes steam engines, Henry's cars, and buildings that look like famous U.S. landmarks.

In 1936, Henry and Edsel began the Ford Foundation. This organization gives money to groups involved in education and research.

Henry died in his home on April 7, 1947. Even after his death, the work of the Ford Foundation continues.

Clara and Henry spent much of their time in the garden at their home, Fair Lane.

Fast Facts about Henry Ford

 Henry tested one of his engines in the kitchen sink.

 In 1918, Henry owned a newspaper called the *Dearborn Examiner*.

 Henry ran for U.S. Senate in 1918. He lost the election.

Dates in Henry Ford's Life

1863—Henry Ford is born July 30 in Dearborn, Michigan.

1876—Henry's mother, Mary Ford, dies.

1879—Henry leaves home to work in Detroit.

1888—Henry marries Clara Bryant.

1896—Henry builds the Quadricycle.

1903—Henry starts the Ford Motor Company.

1908—Henry introduces the Model T.

1913–1914—Henry introduces the assembly line and the $5 daily wage for Ford employees.

1919—Edsel Ford takes over as president of Ford Motor Company.

1929—Henry opens the Henry Ford Museum and Greenfield Village.

1936—Henry and Edsel start the Ford Foundation.

1947—Henry dies April 7 at Fair Lane, his home in Dearborn.

Words to Know

assembly line (uh-SEM-blee LINE)—an arrangement of machines and workers in a factory where work passes from one person or machine to the next until work is complete

complex (KOM-pleks)—a group of buildings that are close together and are used for the same purpose

estate (ess-TATE)—a large area of land, usually with a house on it

foundation (foun-DAY-shuhn)—an organization that gives money to worthwhile causes

mass production (MASS pruh-DUHK-shuhn)—a system of building many things at the same time

minimum (MIN-uh-muhm)—the smallest possible amount

Read More

Ford, Carin T. *Henry Ford: The Car Man.* Famous Inventors. Berkeley Heights, N.J.: Enslow, 2003.

McCarthy, Pat. *Henry Ford: Building Cars for Everyone.* Historical American Biographies. Berkeley Heights, N.J.: Enslow, 2002.

Shuter, Jane. *Henry Ford.* Lives and Times. Chicago: Heinemann, 2001.

Weitzman, David. *Model T: How Henry Ford Built a Legend.* New York: Crown Publishers, 2002.

Useful Addresses

Detroit Historical Museum
5401 Woodward Avenue
Detroit, MI 48202

Henry Ford Museum &
  Greenfield Village
20900 Oakwood Boulevard
Dearborn, MI 48124-4088

Internet Sites

Do you want to find out more about Henry Ford?
Let FactHound, our fact-finding hound dog, do
the research for you.

1) Visit *http://www.facthound.com.*
2) Type in the Book ID number: 0736822232
3) Click on FETCH IT.

FactHound will fetch Internet sites picked by our editors just for you!

Index